W9-BWJ-954

The Library of the Nine Planets™

MARS

Allan B. Cobb

The Rosen Publishing Group, Inc., New York

Published in 2005 by The Rosen Publishing Group, Inc.
29 East 21st Street, New York, NY 10010

Library of Congress Cataloging-in-Publication Data
Cobb, Allan B.
Mars / by Allan B. Cobb.
    p. cm. — (The library of the nine planets)
Summary: Presents scientific discoveries about the atmosphere, size, surface, orbit, and rotation of the Red Planet.
Includes bibliographical references and index.
ISBN 1-4042-0169-6 (lib. bdg.)
1. Mars (Planet)—Juvenile literature. [1. Mars (Planet)] I. Title. II. Series.
QB641.C58 2004
523.43—dc22

2003022511

Manufactured in the United States of America

On the cover: Mars landscape taken by the Mars Exploration Rover *Spirit*.

Contents

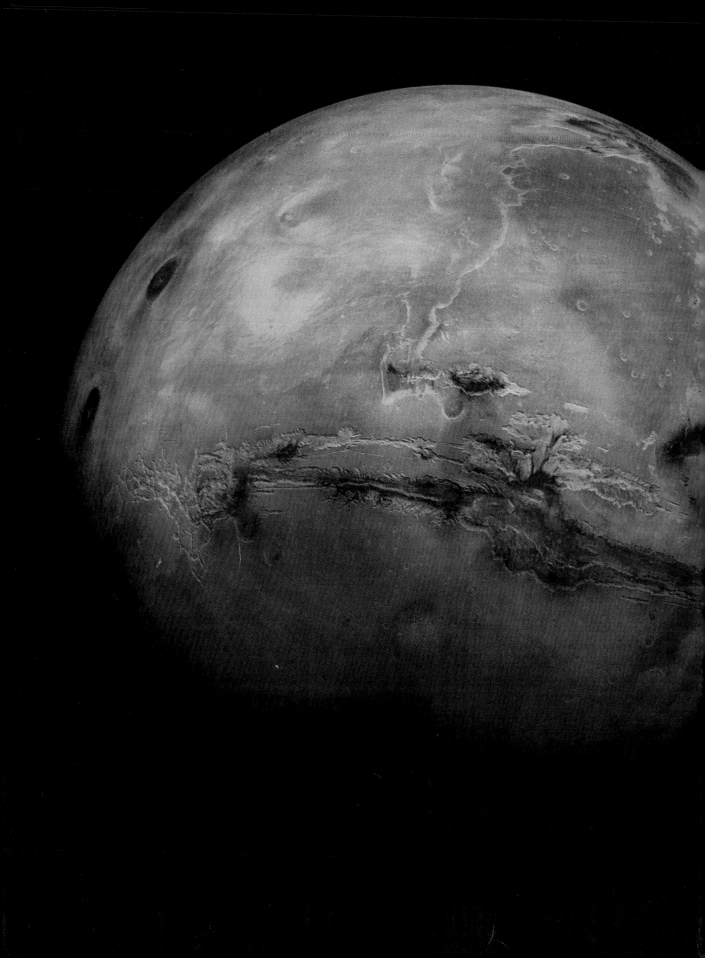

INTRODUCTION

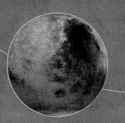

It was a tense night at NASA's Jet Propulsion Laboratory in Pasadena, California, on January 3, 2004. NASA scientists had been holding their breath watching the Mars Exploration Rover *Spirit* descend into the Martian atmosphere.

Then the time came. At 8:29 PM local time, *Spirit* began its descent toward the Martian surface. Of the six-month journey, these final "six minutes of terror" were the most treacherous. *Spirit* had to reduce its speed from 12,000 mph (19,308 km/h) to nearly a full stop.

To do this, it released a parachute and ignited its reversal rockets. Then, just feet above the Martian surface, *Spirit* deployed its air bags, which allowed it to bounce safely for approximately 0.6 miles (1 km) until it came to a stop at approximately 8:45 PM.

The final descent was totally controlled by computers. NASA scientists could do nothing if something went wrong. "All of us are essentially spectators," said Mark Adler, cruise mission manager for *Spirit*, as posted on the NASA Web site. "By then, we have done all we can to assure a safe landing."

And a safe landing it was. There were cheers and champagne at mission control.

This mosaic image *(top)* was taken by the Mars rover *Spirit* upon landing on January 3, 2004. Called a "postcard" by NASA scientists, this was the first image of Mars taken by *Spirit*. Shown at bottom is a scene from the movie *The War of the Worlds*, in which Martians invade Earth. A version of the story was read on a radio broadcast in 1938, and people in the New York City area mistook it for a true news report. These latest images from Mars show us how far we've come from stories like *The War of the Worlds*.

"I really, really like doing this when it works like this," said Richard Cook, NASA's project manager.

Twelve days after landing, *Spirit* rolled off its landing platform and sent full-color images of the planet back to mission control. Then, on January 24, 2004, *Spirit's* twin rover, *Opportunity*, landed on the opposite side of the planet. It landed with similar success and fanfare.

Both rovers sent back some of the clearest images of Mars to date, including some new findings. *Opportunity* went on to find fine layers within bedrock, which suggests that the rock was formed by sediment moved by water. If water once flowed on the planet, there once may have been life on Mars.

Then, on March 2, 2004, *Opportunity* found strong evidence that the area in which it was stationed was soaked with water in the past. The rover found large quantities of minerals and rock formations that could only form in the presence of a great amount of water. "This is the kind of place that would have been suitable for life," said Steven W. Squyres, principal investigator for the mission, as quoted in the *New York Times*.

Even today, after sending spacecraft, landers, and rovers to Mars, we are learning more about the planet on a daily basis. Yet, even with everything we have learned, we are still asking the question, Was there ever life on Mars?

After the successful landings of *Spirit* and *Opportunity*, President George W. Bush announced plans to have astronauts land on Mars by the year 2030. This could be the first time a human would explore the planet and is one of the most ambitious space programs ever proposed.

One

The History of Mars

Mars has captured the attention of humans for thousands of years. From the earliest humans noticing a red star wandering across the sky to scientists poring over data sent back to Earth from satellites, landers, and rovers, Mars has fascinated and intrigued humans.

It is likely that as soon as humans started observing the night sky, they noticed that five objects in particular moved strangely. One of these objects was reddish and made a strange loop in the sky. It would later be discovered that these five bodies were planets.

The ancient Babylonians were the first to record their observations of Mars and did so as early as 400 BC. They called the strange body Nergal, after the great hero and king of conflicts. The ancient Egyptians also described Mars and its movements in the sky. They called it Har Decker, "the red one." The ancient Greeks named the planet Ares for their god of war. The Romans named the planet Mars in honor of their god of agriculture. The Roman god of agriculture later became associated with the Greek god Ares, and Mars became the Roman god of war. The name Mars is the accepted name for the planet today.

Astrologers have also studied the motion of Mars across the sky. They believe that when a person is born, the appearance of Mars in certain constellations influences that person's life.

Mars has been worshiped by many civilizations since ancient times. Shown here is the Temple of Mars in Augustus' Forum in Rome, Italy. It was built by the Romans as a tribute to the victory of Roman emperor Augustus (63 BC–AD 14) over Brutus and Cassius, the murderers of statesman Julius Caesar.

Observing This Unusual Planet

Mars was also used to predict the outcome of events such as wars in many different cultures, including those of the ancient Greeks, the ancient Romans, the Hindus, and the Maya. One reason Mars was used for the prediction of major events in ancient civilizations is that the planet seemed to have an unusual orbit. At times, the planet would appear to move backward in the sky. Scientists studied the motion of Mars and tried to come up with an explanation. In 1609, the German astronomer Johannes Kepler solved the problem.

Kepler discovered that planets did not travel in a perfect circle around the Sun. Instead, they had an elliptical, or oval-shaped, orbit.

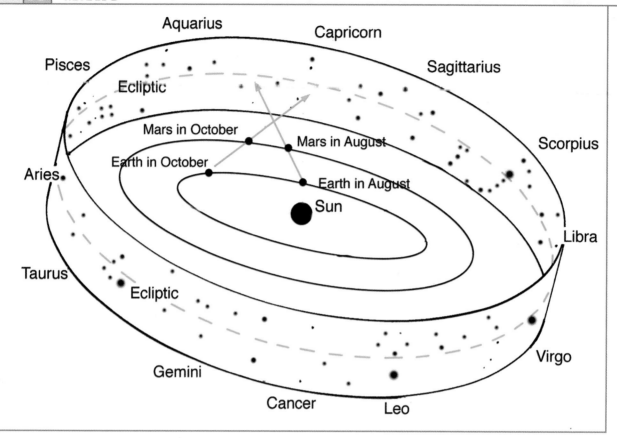

This diagram of the solar system illustrates how retrograde motion works. Since Earth moves in its orbit faster than Mars, it appears to shift from one direction to another in the night sky. Here, Earth is shown as it is positioned in the months of August and October. The arrows indicate the sky gazer's line of sight from Earth. Because Mars appears to move in this strange way, it has always been seen as a different type of object altogether from the stars.

But Mars had a much more elliptical orbit than any of the other known planets. Mars would appear to reverse its course across the sky and make a loop, depending on its location in relation to Earth. This motion is called retrograde motion.

At the same time, the Italian scientist and inventor Galileo Galilei was the first to use a telescope to observe Mars. Galileo's observations indicated that Mars was similar to Earth. As telescopes improved, Mars was observed to have color patterns on its face—clouds, haze, and ice caps—that changed. These observations gave rise to the idea that Mars might be able to support life.

In 1877, the Italian astronomer Giovanni Schiaparelli observed thin, dark lines on Mars. He called them *canali*, the Italian word for "channels." These became widely interpreted as canals, and people believed that a civilization on Mars was using the canals to move water around the planet. The presence of the canals was proved wrong, but the idea of an advanced civilization on Mars continued.

Traveling to This Unusual Planet

In 1964, the United States launched the first spacecraft to fly near Mars. Called *Mariner 4*, it passed within 6,118 miles (9,846 km) of Mars in 1965 and sent back the first detailed pictures of the planet's surface. It showed no canals or civilization. Instead, the pictures showed a landscape of mountains and plains pockmarked with impact craters. Data also indicated that the atmosphere was very thin.

In 1969, *Mariner 6* and *Mariner 7* also flew by Mars. These missions not only sent back pictures of volcanoes, plains, and rugged hills but also showed that Mars was cold.

In 1971, *Mariner 9* became the first spacecraft to orbit Mars. In a little more than a year, *Mariner 9* sent back more than 7,000 images of the surface, analyzed the magnetic field, measured temperatures, and mapped nearly 85 percent of the planet's surface. *Mariner 9* discovered the huge canyon Valles Marineris and the enormous volcano Olympus Mons.

In 1975, the United States launched *Viking 1* and *Viking 2*. Each of these spacecraft was composed of an orbiting satellite and a lander. The satellites would orbit the planet, sending back images and atmospheric data. The landers would land on Mars and analyze the soil for life. *Viking 1* and *Viking 2* landed on different parts of Mars in 1976.

The Mars rover *Spirit* was the first of the two rovers to reach Mars. It landed successfully on January 3, 2004. Shown at left is *Spirit* sitting on its lander in the Jet Propulsion Laboratory in Pasadena, California, before its mission. Its solar panels and wheels are stowed, decreasing its overall size for the half-year-long trip. *Spirit's* predecessor, the *Viking 2* lander, is shown in the inset photo. This image of the surface of Mars was taken on September 25, 1977. It was taken in the Utopia Planitia region of Mars.

Viking 1 landed on the northern plains. It showed a flat surface with rounded rocks. There was red dust everywhere, and the sky was pink. The winds had a speed of about 18 mph (30 km/h). The temperature was 80°F (27°C) in the day and –207°F (–133°C) at night.

Viking 2 landed two months later close to the north pole. The landscape was flat with a few small hills in the distance. The temperatures were similar to those where *Viking 1* landed. Both landers showed nothing moving except small sand dunes. Their experiments did not show any positive signs of life. The Viking orbiters sent back more than 52,000 pictures of the Martian surface.

Little occurred from the end of the Viking program in 1982 until 1996. Between 1988 and 1996, three Russian spacecraft and one NASA spacecraft were launched for Mars. However, all of these missions were unsuccessful.

In 1996, the United States launched the *Mars Pathfinder*. It landed on Mars in 1997. The *Pathfinder* lander also carried a rover called *Sojourner*. The lander sent back 16,500 pictures, and the rover sent back 550. In addition, more than fifteen chemical analyses on soil and extensive data on wind, atmosphere, and temperature were sent back. Much of the data indicates that Mars may well have had water and a denser atmosphere in the past. The *Mars Pathfinder* sent data back to Earth for eighty-three days. This was almost three times as long as it was designed to work.

In 1998, the *Mars Climate Orbiter* was launched by NASA. The goal of the mission was to gather data about the Martian climate over a long period of time. In 1999, the *Mars Climate Orbiter* was lost when it attempted to enter Mars's orbit. Scientists think that miscalculations caused the orbiter to enter and burn up in the thin Martian atmosphere.

When the Mars rover *Spirit* landed on January 3, 2004, its first mission was to visit an impact crater near its landing site. When *Spirit*'s sister rover, *Opportunity*, landed on January 24, 2004, it immediately began studying the soil. Both rovers sent back stunning images but also new findings of strong evidence that a large amount of water once flowed on the planet. If this evidence of water is accurate, then life may once have existed on the planet.

The remote exploration of Mars continues. The past explorations have told us much about Mars, but there are still many questions to be answered.

Looking at the Numbers

Mars is the fourth planet from the Sun in our solar system. The average distance from Mars to the Sun is 142 million miles (229 million km). At its closest point, called the perihelion, Mars is 127 million miles (207 million km) from the Sun. At its farthest point, the aphelion, it is 155 million miles (249 million km) from the Sun.

Because of its elliptical orbit, the velocity of the planet around the Sun changes with its position. The average velocity of Mars is 14.99 miles per second (24.13 km/s). When Mars reaches its perihelion, it travels at 16.47 miles per second (26.50 km/s). At its aphelion, Mars travels at 13.65 miles per second (21.97 km/s).

Mars takes 687 Earth days to orbit the Sun. This means that a Martian year is equivalent to 687 days on Earth, a little less than two Earth years. However, the Martian day, or the time it takes for Mars to make one full rotation on its axis, is almost the same length as an Earth day, twenty-four hours and thirty-seven minutes.

Mars is tilted on its axis at 25 degrees. The tilt, which allows the hemisphere that is tilted toward the Sun to receive more radiation, gives Mars its seasons like on Earth.

The diameter or distance through the center of Mars is 4,220 miles (6,794 km) at the equator. The mass of Mars is 642,000,000,000,000,000,000,000 kilograms. or 6.42×10^{23} kg

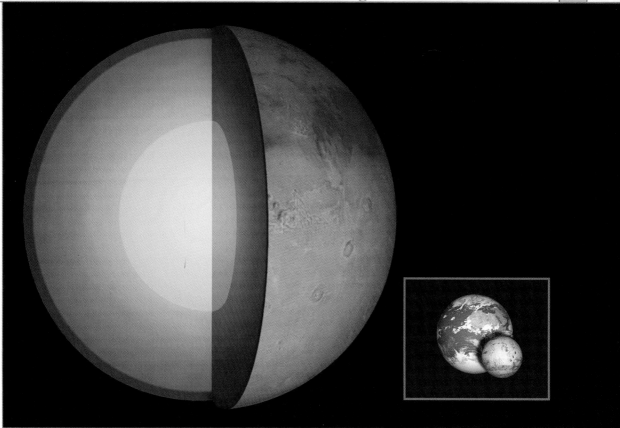

Mars is a rocky planet with several different layers, much like Earth. Shown here is a cross section of the various layers beneath the Martian surface. In yellow is the core, which is made of molten iron. Outside the core is a thick mantle, which is shown in orange. Outside the mantle is the crust, shown in brown. In the lower right-hand corner is an artist's rendition of Earth *(background)* and Mars *(foreground)*, showing their relative sizes.

in scientific notation. Mass is a measure of the amount of matter in an object.

The average density of Mars is 3.94 g/cm³. Mars has a volume of 1.63×10^{11} km³. This makes Mars about half the diameter, one-tenth the mass, and about three-quarters the density of Earth.

Density is a measure of the amount of matter in a certain volume. Density is one way that planets of different sizes can be compared. Because Mars is smaller, has less mass, and is less dense than Earth, the strength of the gravity on Mars is also less than it is on Earth.

Because the gravity on Mars is only about one-third as strong as Earth's gravity, you would weigh only about one-third as much. To figure out your weight on Mars, just multiply it by 0.37. So if you weigh 100 pounds (37 kg) on Earth, you would weigh only 37 pounds (14 kg) on Mars.

The Mineral Resources of Mars

The red color of Mars is due to iron in the soil and rocks. The iron has reacted with oxygen in the atmosphere to form iron oxide, or rust. This red color is common in the dust, soil, and many of the rocks on Mars.

Mars is made up of a number of different elements. Based on soil and rock analyses by the *Mars Pathfinder*, the major elements on the surface of Mars are oxygen, silicon, iron, magnesium, calcium, and sodium. Many other common elements were also found. Based on the complex geologic history of the planet, it is likely that many of the minerals found on Mars can also be found on Earth.

One of the biggest debates about Mars is whether there is a large amount of water on the planet. Most scientists believe that there was in the past because of *Opportunity*'s March 2, 2004, discovery. But the big question still remains: What happened to the water? Some scientists believe that most of the water was lost with the Martian atmosphere, which was somehow mostly stripped from the planet.

The atmosphere that remains on Mars has been well studied. It is thin and made up of carbon dioxide (95.3 percent), nitrogen (2.7 percent), argon (1.6 percent), traces of oxygen, and water vapor. The average atmospheric pressure on Mars is less than 1 percent of Earth's.

This image of the Martian landscape was taken by the rover *Spirit* just before it rolled off its lander in January 2004. Scientists were eager to study the rocks. Unlike the soil, the rocks are considered little time capsules that hold information about how they were formed. By studying the rocks, scientists can gather information about past erosion, the composition of Mars, and much more, all of which can help them piece together a picture of what Mars was once like.

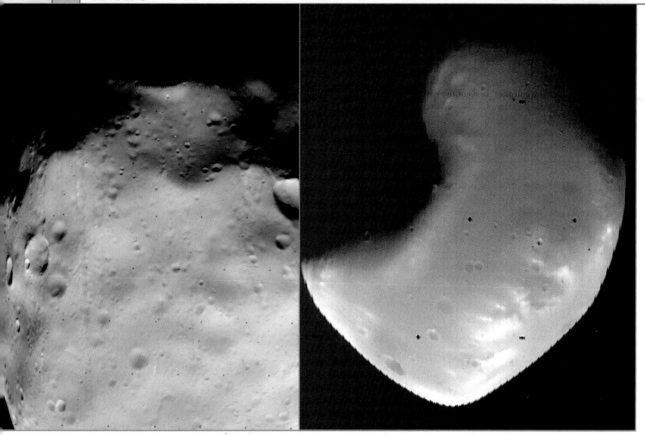

Shown on the left is an image of the Martian moon Phobos taken by *Viking 1* on February 19, 1977. The image was taken from a distance of about 373 miles (600 km). Since it doesn't have an atmosphere, Phobos has many visible impact craters from objects that were able to reach the surface without burning up. Pictured on the right is the Martian moon Deimos. The moon's smooth appearance is a result of the dust that blankets the surface. This image was taken by *Viking 2* from a distance of about 870 miles (1,400 km).

The Moons of Mars

Mars has two small moons called Phobos and Deimos. The larger moon, Phobos, passes across the Martian sky from west to east twice a day and looks about half as big as the full moon does on Earth. Phobos is so close to Mars that it is not even visible from the poles. Phobos is slowly moving closer to Mars and is predicted to spiral into the planet in 50 million to 100 million years.

Phobos is only about 3,700 miles (6,000 km) from Mars. Deimos is much farther from Mars and looks like a small dot of light in the sky that passes from east to west. Deimos is about 12,400 miles (20,000 km) from Mars.

Phobos is a small, dark body without an atmosphere. It may also be one of the driest moons in the solar system. Phobos appears to have survived a massive impact from a large asteroid, which seems to have fractured the moon's interior. The impact gouged a huge crater and may have caused deep grooves that radiate from the crater.

Deimos is smaller than Phobos. It's covered with powdery dust that could be more than 330 feet (100 m) thick. The surface shows the tips of giant boulders sticking out of the dusty surface. Scientists believe that the dust is from billions of years of meteorite impacts, which pulverized the moon's surface.

Because neither of the moons is spherical in shape, some scientists believe that Phobos and Deimos were actually passing asteroids that were pulled into orbit around Mars billions of years ago. Other scientists think that either the moons were formed at the same time as Mars or they are remnants of a larger moon that was shattered by a collision with an asteroid or meteorite.

Three

The Martian Landscape

Even though Mars is much smaller and colder than Earth, the two planets have many similarities. Mars has many different types of landforms. These include volcanoes, impact craters, canyons, dune fields, and channels that may have been formed by flowing water. Because there is no water on the planet's surface now, these landforms are well preserved.

Prominent Surface Features

The largest volcano in the solar system is on Mars. This volcano, named Olympus Mons, stands 17 miles (27 km) high. If this volcano were on Earth, it would cover an area the size of the state of New Mexico and stand three times taller than the tallest mountain on Earth, Mount Everest.

The "grand canyon" of Mars is called Valles Marineris. Valles Marineris is a series of canyons that stretches more than 2,500 miles (4,000 km) long. If this canyon were on Earth, it would stretch from New York to Los Angeles and would be up to three times deeper than the Grand Canyon.

Mars also has a huge depression called Hellas Planitia. Hellas Planitia is the oldest impact crater in the southern hemisphere. Scientists believe that this huge impact basin was formed when an asteroid collided with Mars about 3 billion years ago.

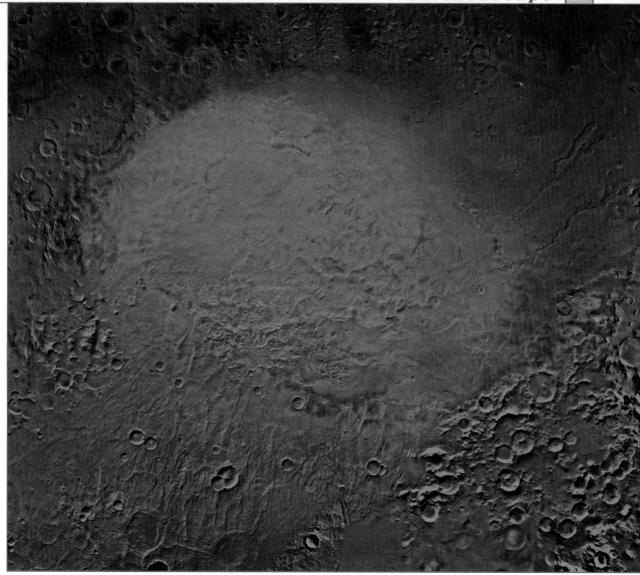

The circular formation in the landscape shown here is the Hellas Planitia impact crater. To get a sense of its size, the circular formations surrounding Hellas Planitia are impact craters as well. Hellas Planitia, which is 1,119 miles (1,800 km) across, is the largest depression known to exist on Mars.

The Plains

The northern hemisphere of Mars is mostly plains. The plains are believed to be rather young because the area lacks many impact craters. This suggests that the exposed surface was formed somewhat recently and has not had many impacts.

Other plains, such as the Lunae Planum, have an interesting texture and fracture pattern. These plains are assumed to be volcanic, but scientists are not certain how they formed. Scientists think that freezing water may have helped to make the fracture patterns.

Some plains areas, particularly near the north pole, have extensive sand dune fields. The dunes form patterns just like those seen on Earth in the Sahara Desert. The winds on Mars constantly change the shapes and patterns of the dunes.

The Highlands

In contrast to the relatively flat plains are the rocky highlands. The highlands cover almost the entire southern hemisphere and actually make up about two-thirds of the planet's surface. Scientists believe the highlands represent a much older surface than the plains.

The cratered highlands of Mars also show a number of other features. Aside from Olympus Mons, many other volcanoes exist. These volcanoes are among the largest known in the solar system. No one has seen the volcanoes erupt, and it is believed that they have been dormant for a long time.

The craters of the highlands are interesting to scientists because they provide clues about the past climate. Most of the

A Close Flyby

On August 27, 2003, Earth and Mars were 35 million miles (56 million km) apart, the closest they had been in almost 60,000 years. Mars and Earth will not be this close to each other again until the year 2287.

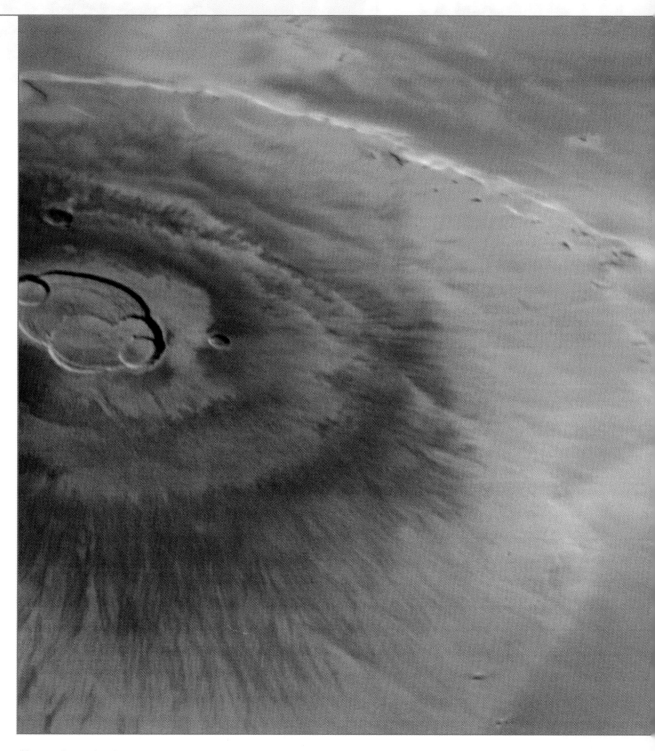

Shown here is the enormous volcano Olympus Mons. Though it is three times taller than Mount Everest, the tallest mountain on Earth, it covers an area the size of New Mexico. This makes it extremely flat, so much so that it would be possible to walk up its slope. This image was taken by the *Mars Global Surveyor* orbiter from a height of 560 miles (900 km).

This mosaic image, taken by *Spirit* on January 18–19, 2004, shows how barren the landscape of Mars is. In the foreground is the unfolded lander. The landing site is in Gusev Crater. The site was named Columbia Memorial Station in honor of the astronauts who perished in the *Columbia* shuttle disaster approximately one year before on February 1, 2003.

craters show signs of erosion. The craters lack sharply defined edges, and the debris ejected from the craters appears to have eroded. Scientists believe that this evidence supports the idea that Mars had a warmer climate and surface water at one time. The warmer, wetter climate would have caused erosion, which would have smoothed out the edges of the impact craters.

The surface of Mars is probably the most similar to Earth's surface. The landscape of Mars shows that it has had a complex geologic history. Volcanoes are responsible for creating most of the landforms, and wind and water have been key elements in eroding these landforms.

Four

The Unique Weather

The Martian climate has changed greatly throughout the history of the planet. Many of the geologic features of Mars show that liquid water likely caused erosion. For liquid water to have existed on Mars, the climate in the past had to have been much different than it is today. Today, the atmosphere is too thin and the planet is too cold to support liquid water on the surface.

The Atmosphere

The Martian atmospheric pressure averages about 1 percent of the atmospheric pressure on Earth. But many scientists think that the Martian atmosphere in the past was much different than it is today. Because so many geologic features show evidence of erosion by water, scientists think that the atmosphere was much thicker.

It is also possible that the atmosphere contained more carbon dioxide and possibly other greenhouse gases. The greenhouse gases allowed the atmosphere to trap heat and warm the planet to the point where liquid water existed and possibly formed rivers, lakes, and oceans.

Scientists still do not have an explanation as to what happened to the ancient Martian atmosphere or the water. This scientific debate will likely continue far into the future as more and more data is recovered from Mars.

This image of Melas Chasma was taken by the *Mars Odyssey* spacecraft. The different colors indicate the differences in temperature between day and night. The daytime temperatures range from -31°F (-35°C) in white to 23°F (-5°C) in black. The range of nighttime temperatures is represented in color.

The Climate

The Martian climate is highly variable. This is due mainly to three factors: the thin atmosphere, Mars's highly elliptical orbit, and the interaction between dust and water ice clouds. Water ice clouds are similar to cirrus clouds on Earth because they are composed of ice crystals from water. The thin atmosphere of Mars causes the planet to heat up and cool down quickly.

Also, unlike Earth, Mars lacks large oceans, which hold heat and moderate temperatures. During the day, the Sun quickly heats up the surface. At night, the land quickly cools. This causes the temperature difference between night and day to vary greatly. The average temperature on Mars is –67°F (–55°C). However, the temperature ranges from –207°F (–133°C) at the poles in the winter to 80°F (27°C) during the summer.

The highly elliptical orbit of Mars also contributes to the extreme temperature differences between summer and winter. The difference between the shortest and longest distances between Mars and the Sun varies by about 20 percent. (Summer in the southern hemisphere occurs when Mars is at its closest point to the Sun because the southern hemisphere is tilted toward the Sun. Summer in the northern hemisphere occurs when Mars is at its farthest point from the Sun and the northern hemisphere is tilted toward the Sun.)

When Mars is closest to the Sun, it receives 40 percent more of the Sun's energy than it does at its farthest point, causing higher temperatures. These increased temperatures cause massive dust storms. Some of these dust storms are small, while others can spread over the entire surface of the planet. The increased dust in the atmosphere absorbs even more heat and raises temperatures across the entire planet.

The dust that causes the increased temperatures does not last throughout the entire year. As Mars moves farther from the Sun, the planet receives less solar radiation. The decreased solar radiation slightly decreases the temperature of the atmosphere, causing water clouds to form across the planet. These clouds reflect solar energy and start a rapid cooling across the planet. As the temperature drops, the water droplets in the clouds begin to freeze around dust particles. This causes the dust particles to drop out of the atmosphere. The combination of the clouds and the clear atmosphere causes temperatures to drop significantly.

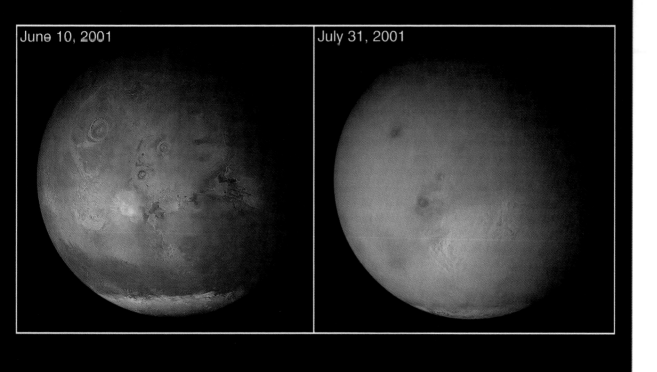

June 10, 2001   July 31, 2001

These images of Mars, taken by *Mars Global Surveyor*, are a few of the many that the craft takes every day to track the changes in weather on Mars. The image on the left, taken on June 10, 2001, shows ice in the southern hemisphere. Winter was turning to spring, and the cold air from the south pole was moving northward. As this was happening, dust storms began to pick up, eventually covering the entire planet in dust, as shown in the July 31, 2001, image.

The Weather

The weather on Mars is as variable as the climate. Sometimes, the sky is pink from the dust in the atmosphere. At other times, the sky is dark blue with brilliant white clouds. When the sky is pink, the weather is warm and the temperature might be 80°C (27°F). When the dust clears, the temperature can drop to −207°F (−133°C). These extremes can happen over the span of a couple of days.

Sometimes, swirling winds cause dust devils—small, tornado-like storms—on the Martian surface. These dust devils may grow to 1.2 miles (2 km) in diameter. These are short-lived weather features that seldom last for more than a few hours.

Near the equator, localized dust storms occur. A typical dust storm would cover about 390,000 square miles (1 million square km) or about one and a half times the size of Texas. The dust storms have wind speeds of 33 to 66 mph (53 to 106 km/h). These dust storms usually last only a few days. However, they can sometimes continue to expand, and eventually the entire surface of the planet can be covered with a huge dust storm. These storms sometimes happen once or twice a year, while in other years they do not happen at all. Scientists do not have enough information to understand what causes these dust storms to start or stop.

Another unusual type of storm on Mars is the cyclone. These swirling masses of water clouds are similar to hurricanes on Earth. The largest Martian cyclone detected so far was about 900 to 1,100 miles (1,500 to 1,800 km) in diameter. The eye of the storm was 200 miles (320 km) across. So far, cyclones have only been detected in the northern hemisphere during the summer. Scientists are not sure how these storms form or why they form only in the northern hemisphere.

Scientists are trying to understand the weather and weather patterns on Mars to assist with future explorations. When a lander touches down on Mars, it is important that it be engineered to withstand the day and night temperatures and the rapid heating and cooling. Also, the dust can play an important factor in the success of the mission. A dust storm can blanket an area with thick dust. The landers use solar panels to generate electricity. If the dust forms a thick layer over the solar panels, the lander will not be able to charge its batteries and function.

This high-resolution image taken by *Spirit* on January 14, 2004, shows a patch of soil in Gusev Crater, not far from the rover's landing site. Scientists studied the soil using nearly all of the instruments on *Spirit*'s examination arm. They made some puzzling findings, including discovering that the soil is much heavier than they expected.

Life on Mars

One of the greatest debates in planetary science is whether life exists on Mars. Of all the planets other than Earth, Mars is the most likely to harbor life. Liquid water is essential for life as we know it, and Mars appears to have or have had water.

The first attempt to settle the debate was in the 1970s with the Viking landers. They performed a series of carefully designed experiments. Soil samples were mixed with water and nutrients and warmed to see if life was present. The results of the tests were not clear. However, thirty years later, most scientists now believe that the tests showed no signs of life. The soil samples for testing were taken at only two different locations. The tests have not settled the debate.

The debate over life on Mars heated up on August 6, 1996. A group of NASA scientists announced that they had found carbon compounds possibly formed by living organisms in a Martian meteorite found in Antarctica. The team examined the meteorite, called ALH840001, and reported that they had found organic compounds and fossilized nanobacteria. Nanobacteria are a recently discovered type of bacteria that are much smaller than other bacteria. Some scientists even wonder if nanobacteria are actually living organisms. The fossilized nanobacteria in the meteorite are similar in size and shape to nanobacteria found on Earth. The debate still continues about what was found in this meteorite.

Future missions to Mars will be designed to test new locations and use new methods to detect life, like the *Spirit* and *Opportunity* rovers. As an example, on March 2, 2004, *Opportunity* found certain minerals that suggested that a good amount of water may have once been present on the planet. And with water comes life. Scientists believe that if there is indeed life on Mars, it will be found underground near water and in temperature conditions more stable than those on the surface.

Scientists are refining their techniques to search for these types of life in extreme environments on Earth. The extreme environments on Earth are in hot springs, lakes deep inside glaciers, and caves. Scientists are finding life in these extreme environments on Earth so they are hoping that their work can be used on Mars to explore the extreme environments there.

The Present and the Future

With the January 2004 rover missions, the exploration of Mars continues. The successes of the previous missions have created enthusiasm to continue exploration.

Recent Mars Missions

NASA's *Mars Global Surveyor* was launched on November 7, 1996, and entered orbit around Mars on September 12, 1997. The primary mission was to take high-resolution photographic images of the surface, map the surface for elevation and mineral distribution, record Martian weather, and measure the magnetic field. The primary mission was completed on January 31, 2001.

Now, *Mars Global Surveyor* has begun its extended mission, which includes taking additional high-resolution photographs of selected features from different angles in orbit to make three-dimensional representations of these images. The extended mission will continue as long as the satellite is functional. Daily weather data continues to be collected so that scientists may better understand how the weather changes. Scientists also monitor storms to help them better understand how they form. The cameras are also recording the same features over and over to determine if erosion is still occurring and, if so, at what rate.

NASA's *Mars Odyssey* was launched on April 7, 2001, and entered orbit around Mars on October 24, 2001. Since that

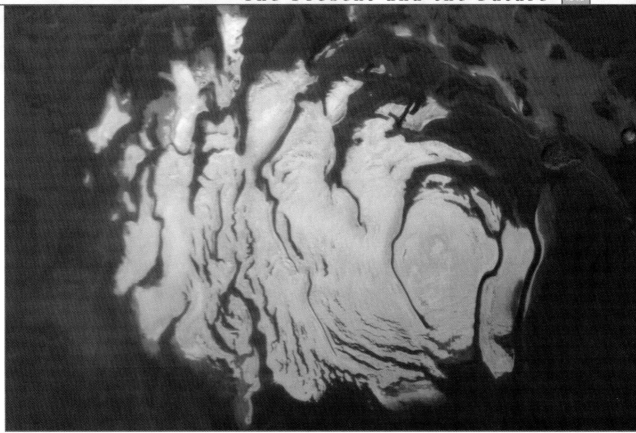

Shown here is the south pole of Mars. This image was taken by the *Mars Global Surveyor* on April 17, 2000. In the winter and early spring, the south polar cap is completely covered by frost. In the summer, the time when this image was taken, the cap shrinks to its smallest size.

time, the satellite has been recording information on where water might exist. The satellite is able to search the entire surface of Mars for water up to 3 feet (1 m) below the surface. In addition, the satellite measures the radiation that Mars receives over long periods of time so that potential effects on humans who might explore or live on the planet can be determined. The satellite is also able to act as a communications relay for future projects.

Mars Express is a joint project between NASA and the European Space Agency. It was launched on June 2, 2003, and entered orbit around Mars on December 24, 2003. When *Mars Express* entered orbit, it also sent a lander, *Beagle 2*, to the surface. The mission of the lander was to conduct detailed tests on the soil and rocks. *Beagle 2* was set to land on December 25, 2003. Unfortunately, the spacecraft failed to return a signal. The orbiter continued mapping for subsurface water as well as data about the Martian atmosphere. The satellite gathered more information on the structure and geology of Mars.

NASA's Mars Exploration Rover mission has landed two rovers on Mars. The mission was launched in two parts. *Spirit* was launched on June 19, 2003, and *Opportunity* was launched on July 7, 2003. The landers touched down in January 2004 on opposite sides of Mars. After landing, the rovers moved around and explored the surface of Mars near the landing sites. Each of the landers then started a mission that lasted for several months.

During the day, solar cells charged batteries and provided power for the rovers. The rovers moved around under the control of scientists on Earth. The rovers performed studies on rocks and soil to determine the minerals they contain. These studies provided scientists with information about how the rocks were formed and whether the rocks are igneous (formed from molten magma), sedimentary (formed by deposition), or metamorphic (formed by heat and pressure). The rovers also searched for iron minerals. *Opportunity* discovered minerals and rock formations that strongly indicate that water once flowed in the Meridiani Planum plain. This information is continuing to help scientists understand the role that water has played on Mars.

Future Mars Missions

NASA's *Mars Reconnaissance Orbiter* is scheduled to launch in August 2005. This satellite will carry the highest resolution camera ever sent to another planet. Previous satellite cameras have been

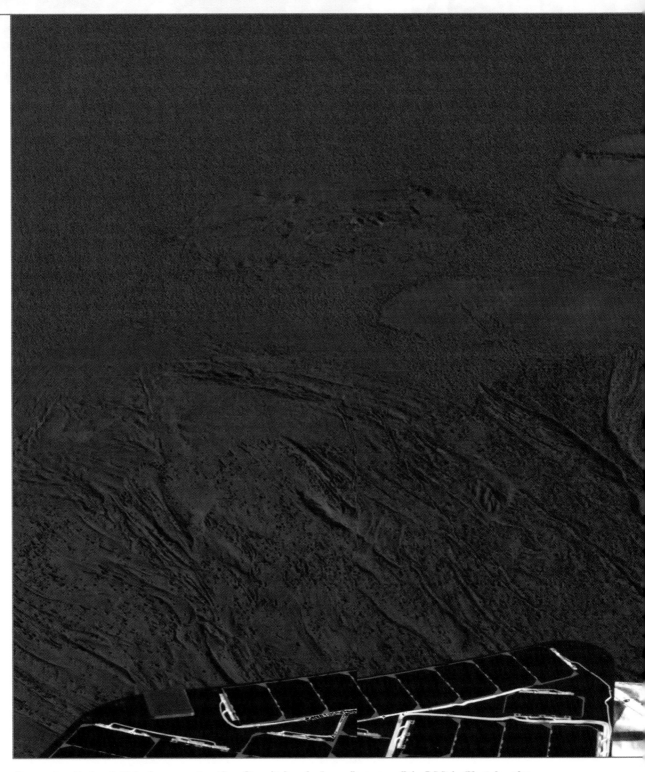

Opportunity took this image shortly after it landed on January 24, 2004. Shot by the rover's panoramic camera, it is one of the first images *Opportunity* sent back. It shows the landscape at the Meridiani Planum region. Unlike images taken by its sister rover, *Spirit*, this picture reveals a relatively flat and smooth landscape. The area lacks the rough soil and rocks found near *Spirit*'s landing site.

able to see only objects at least the size of a dinner table. The camera on the *Mars Reconnaissance Orbiter* will be able to see objects the size of a dinner plate. This will give scientists a closer view of geologic features as well as provide detailed photographs of future landing sites. Instruments on the satellite will continue the mapping of minerals on the surface and provide information about atmospheric dust. The satellite will also serve as a communications link to Earth for future missions to Mars.

NASA's Phoenix mission is the first in a new series of missions called Scout missions. Scout missions are missions that have some kind of specific goal to learn more about one aspect of Mars. Each Scout mission will use a variety of techniques to accomplish its objectives. Not all of the Scout missions are defined yet, and they may be based on new information or new techniques as they are developed. The Phoenix mission is planned for 2008. Its lander will land near the north pole on Mars. A robotic arm will scoop up a soil sample and measure the amount of carbon dioxide, water, and minerals in the sample. This will help scientists understand the role of water and carbon dioxide on the past climate of Mars.

A second sample will be scooped up and mixed with water. The water will then be analyzed to see what happens. This test will tell scientists what happens if the soil gets wet. Knowing whether the soil is highly acidic or basic, contains strong oxidizers, or contains too much salt will help scientists understand if life is able to exist in the wet soil.

Other proposed Scout missions will perform other functions, such as launching small remote-controlled airplanes or balloons. Airplanes could carry instruments to study the weather and cameras for taking detailed photographs. They could also fly around and zoom in on specific objects.

Adirondack ("they of the great rocks"), the name that scientists gave to the rock shown here, is the first rock that was studied by *Spirit*. *Spirit* traveled over the sandy terrain of Gusev Crater to arrive at the football-sized rock on January 18, 2004. Scientists chose this particular rock because it was relatively smooth and free of dust, which made it perfect for grinding for the study.

Balloons have an advantage over remote-controlled planes in that they can stay aloft much longer. A disadvantage of balloons, however, is that they cannot be controlled and will move only where the wind blows them.

Scout missions could also use small landers to perform specific tests on minerals, the atmosphere, rocks, and soil or to continue in the search for life. The goal of the Scout missions is to provide scientific data at a minimal cost. As a result, the equipment carried on the mission—a plane, balloon, or small lander—must be compact and light.

NASA and other space agencies have several other plans for missions. Many of these missions are joint ventures between NASA and other countries. None of these missions is funded or scheduled, but work on them continues.

One of the missions planned by NASA is to send a laboratory to Mars. The Mars Science Laboratory will use "smart lander" technology. The lander will have cameras and sonar that guide the craft to avoid obstacles as it approaches the surface. If this technology works, it will be used on future lander missions. The Mars Science Laboratory would carry out scientific experiments over the course of several years.

Another future mission is a sample return mission. In this mission, a lander would collect samples of rocks or soil on Mars and then launch these items back into space for return to Earth. The samples would give scientists an opportunity to study the planet's rocks in much greater detail than would be possible in a remote laboratory. Current plans for a return sample mission are proposed for 2014. However, as funding and priorities change, the mission could happen sooner, later, or not at all.

Another proposed project would be to send a miniature drilling rig to Mars to drill several hundred meters into the crust to look at the structural geology. This mission has a number of obstacles to overcome before it can be considered.

Human Exploration on Mars

Sending astronauts to Mars is one of the ultimate goals of the NASA space program. However, sending astronauts to Mars has many logistical complications. The first obstacle is the fact that it takes six to ten months to reach Mars from Earth with a return trip of the same length of time. Supplying astronauts with food and water for such a trip would be difficult but not impossible.

Then, the problem becomes what to do with the astronauts when they get to Mars. The atmosphere cannot support them, so they must have oxygen. One of the ideas to overcome this problem is to send a habitat lander to Mars years ahead of astronauts. When the lander lands on Mars, it could start removing what little oxygen is in the Martian atmosphere and store it. Water could be obtained either the same way or through drilling into under-ground deposits. The astronauts could then land on Mars and move into the habitat.

Showing that scientists are learning something new about Mars every day, the Mars rover *Opportunity* discovered this section of rock, called El Capitan, at Meridiani Planum on March 1, 2004. The chemical composition of the rock indicates that this region of Mars was once soaked with water, which raises the possibility that life may have once existed here.

These plans will be tested within the next few decades. With his announcement on January 14, 2004, to send astronauts to Mars by the year 2030, President George W. Bush opened up a universe of possibilities for the space program. The mission would be difficult. However, if a human mission to Mars succeeded, it would mark a new chapter in space exploration. We would not only be able to search for extraterrestrial life on the Red Planet, we would also be able to tell if Mars could one day be a home for human beings.

Timeline of Exploration and Discovery

400 BC: The ancient Babylonians first describe observations of Mars.

1609: German astronomer Johannes Kepler solves the mystery of retrograde motion by looking at Mars.

1877: Italian astronomer Giovanni Schiaparelli notices dark lines on the Martian surface and calls them channels.

1964: The United States launches *Mariner 4*, the first spacecraft to fly near Mars.

1969: The United States launches *Mariner 6* and *Mariner 7* to fly by Mars.

1971: *Mariner 9* becomes the first spacecraft to orbit Mars.

1975: The United States launches *Viking 1* and *Viking 2* to test the Martian soil for life.

1996: The United States' *Mars Pathfinder* is launched. NASA's *Mars Global Surveyor* enters Mars's orbit on September 12.

1997: *Pathfinder* lands on Mars.

1998: The *Mars Climate Orbiter* is launched by NASA.

2001: The primary mission of *Mars Global Surveyor* is completed on January 31. NASA's *Mars Odyssey* is launched on April 7 and enters orbit around Mars on October 24.

2003: *Mars Express*, a joint project between NASA and the European Space Agency, is launched on June 2 and enters orbit on December 24. The *Spirit* rover is launched on June 19. The *Opportunity* rover is launched on July 7.

2004: The *Spirit* rover lands on Mars on January 3. The *Opportunity* rover lands on Mars on January 24. On March 2, *Opportunity* finds strong evidence that large amounts of water once existed on the planet.

2005: NASA's *Mars Reconnaissance Orbiter* is scheduled to launch in August.

2008: NASA's Phoenix mission is scheduled to launch.

2014: A sample return mission is scheduled to launch.

Glossary

aphelion The farthest point from the Sun in an elliptical orbit.

axis A straight line around which a body rotates.

climate The average weather conditions in an area over time.

diameter The distance of a straight line through the center of an object.

elliptical Having a path shaped like an oval.

erosion The moving or transporting of material by the action of wind, water, gravity, or ice.

gravity The force that exists between two or more objects with mass.

greenhouse gases Atmospheric gases that trap heat in a planet's atmosphere and prevent it from escaping into space.

igneous Formed by the cooling of magma.

impact crater A circular crater formed when a meteorite or asteroid strikes a surface.

lander A space vehicle, which often contains a rover, that is designed to land on a celestial body.

orbit The path of one body around another.

oxidizer A substance that combines with oxygen.

perihelion The closest point to the Sun in an elliptical orbit.

retrograde motion Reverse motion through the sky relative to typical motion.

rover A vehicle that is designed to explore the terrain of planets other than Earth.

scientific notation A mathematical system that uses an exponent to show how many decimal places a number has.

water vapor Water in a gaseous state.

Ames Research Center
Moffet Field, CA 94035
(650) 604-5000
Web site: http://www.arc.nasa.gov

Goddard Space Flight Center
Code 130
Office of Public Affairs
Greenbelt, MD 20771
(301) 286-8955
e-mail: gsfcpao@pop100.gsfc.nasa.gov
Web site: http://www.gsfc.nasa.gov

Jet Propulsion Laboratory
4800 Oak Grove Drive
Pasadena, CA 91109
(818) 354-4321
Web site: http://www.jpl.nasa.gov

National Aeronautics and Space Administration (NASA)
NASA Headquarters
Washington, DC 20546-0001
(202) 358-0000
Web site: http://www.nasa.gov

The Planetary Society
65 North Catalina Avenue
Pasadena, CA 91106-2301
(626) 793-5100
e-mail: tps@planetary.org

Smithsonian National Air and Space Museum
Seventh Street and Independence Avenue SW
Washington, DC 20560
(202) 357-2700
Web site: http://www.nasm.si.edu

Web Sites

Due to the changing nature of Internet links, the Rosen Publishing Group, Inc., has developed an online list of Web sites related to the subject of this book. This site is updated regularly. Please use this link to access the list:

http://www.rosenlinks.com/lnp/mars

For Further Reading

Bergin, Mark. *Exploration of Mars* (Fast Forward). New York: Franklin Watts, 2001.

Getz, David. *Life on Mars* (A Redfeather Book). New York: Henry Holt & Company, Inc., 1997.

Gifford, Clive. *How to Live on Mars*. New York: Franklin Watts, 2001.

Powers, Robert M. *Mars: Our Future on the Red Planet*. Boston: Houghton Mifflin Company, 1986.

Ride, Sally, and Tam O'Shaughnessy. *The Mystery of Mars*. New York: Crown Publishing Group, 1999.

Bibliography

Boyce, Joseph M. *The Smithsonian Book of Mars*. Washington, DC: Smithsonian Institution Press, 2003.

Cattermole, Peter John. *Mars: The Mystery Unfolds*. New York: Oxford University Press, 2001.

Hartmann, William K. *A Traveler's Guide to Mars*. New York: Workman Publishing Company, 2003.

Sheehan, William. *The Planet Mars: A History of Observation & Discovery*. Tuscon, AZ: University of Arizona Press, 1996.

Sheehan, William, and Stephen James O'Meara. *Mars: The Lure of the Red Planet*. Amherst, NY: Prometheus Books, 2001.

Zubrin, Robert, and Richard Wagner. *The Case for Mars: The Plan to Settle the Red Planet*. New York: Free Press, 1996.

Index

About the Author

Allan B. Cobb is a freelance science editor who lives in central Texas. He has written books, articles, radio scripts, and educational materials concerning different aspects of science. When not writing about science, he enjoys traveling, camping, hiking, and exploring caves.

Photo Credits

Cover © NASA/Roger Ressmeyer/Corbis; pp. 4–5 NASA/USGS; pp. 6 (top), 12 NASA/JPL; p. 6 (bottom) © Hulton Archive/Getty Images, Inc.; p. 9 © Angelo Hornak/Corbis; p. 10 © Jon Lomberg/Science Photo Library; p. 12 (inset) NASA/GSFC; p. 15 © Mark Garlick/Science Photo Library; pp. 17, 24, 30, 35, 37 NASA/JPL/Cornell; p. 18 NSSDC/NASA; p. 21 © U.S. Geological Survey/JPL/NASA; pp. 23, 28, 33 © NASA/JPL/Malin Space Science Systems; p. 26 © NASA/JPL/Arizona State University.

Designer: Thomas Forget; Editor: Nicholas Croce